[illegible] White

from Gordon W. Lloyd.

Jan. 1st 186[illegible]

GERTRUDE OF WYOMING
BY
CAMPBELL
ILLUSTRATED
D. APPLETON & Co. NEW YORK.

# GERTRUDE OF WYOMING;

OR,

# THE PENNSYLVANIAN COTTAGE.

BY

THOMAS CAMPBELL.

WITH THIRTY-FIVE ILLUSTRATIONS,

ENGRAVED BY THE BROTHERS DALZIEL.

NEW YORK:

D. APPLETON & CO 346 AND 348, BROADWAY.

1858.

Alfred H. White
gt.
4-19-1923

LONDON:
PRINTED BY RICHARD CLAY,
BREAD STREET HILL.

# ADVERTISEMENT.

---

Most of the popular histories of England, as well as of the American war, give an authentic account of the desolation of Wyoming, in Pennsylvania, which took place in 1778, by an incursion of the Indians. The Scenery and Incidents of the following Poem are connected with that event. The testimonies of historians and travellers concur in describing the infant colony as one of the happiest spots of human existence, for the hospitable and innocent manners of the inhabitants, the beauty of the country, and the luxuriant fertility of the soil and climate. In an evil hour, the junction of European with Indian arms converted this terrestrial paradise into a frightful waste. Mr. Isaac Weld informs us, that the ruins of many of the villages, perforated with balls, and bearing marks of conflagration, were still preserved by the recent inhabitants, when he travelled through America in 1796.

# LIST OF ILLUSTRATIONS,

## ENGRAVED BY THE BROTHERS DALZIEL.

---

PART I
Macquoid del

ON Susquehana's side, fair Wyoming,

Although the wild-flower on thy ruin'd wall

And roofless homes a sad remembrance bring
Of what thy gentle people did befal,
Yet thou wert once the loveliest land of all
That see the Atlantic wave their morn restore.
Sweet land ! may I thy lost delights recal,
And paint thy Gertrude in her bowers of yore,
Whose beauty was the love of Pennsylvania's shore !

II.

It was beneath thy skies that, but to prune
His Autumn fruits, or skim the light canoe,
Perchance, along thy river calm at noon,
The happy shepherd swain had nought to do—
From morn till evening's sweeter pastime grew
Their timbrel, in the dance of forests brown,
When lovely maidens prankt in flowret new ;
And ay, those sunny mountains halfway down
Would echo flagelet from some romantic town.

Then, where of Indian hills the daylight takes
His leave, how might you the flamingo see

Disporting like a meteor on the lakes—
And playful squirrel on his nut-grown tree :
And every sound of life was full of glee,
From merry mock-bird's song,[1] or hum of men,
While heark'ning, fearing nought their revelry,
The wild deer arch'd his neck from glades, and then,
Unhunted, sought his woods and wilderness again.

IV.

And scarce had Wyoming of war or crime
Heard but in transatlantic story rung ;
For here the exile met from ev'ry clime,
And spoke in friendship ev'ry distant tongue :
Men from the blood of warring Europe sprung,
Were but divided by the running brook ;
And happy where no Rhenish trumpet sung,
On plains no sieging mine's volcano shook,
The blue-eyed German changed his sword to pruning-hook.

V.

Nor far some Andalusian saraband
Would sound to many a native rondelay.
But who is he that yet a dearer land
Remembers, over hills and far away?
Green Albyn![2] what though he no more survey
Thy ships at anchor on the quiet shore,
Thy pellochs[3] rolling from the mountain bay,
Thy lone sepulchral cairn upon the moor,
And distant isles that hear the loud Corbrechtan roar![4]

VI.

Alas! poor Caledonia's mountaineer,
That Want's stern edict e'er, and feudal grief,
Had forced him from a home he loved so dear!
Yet found he here a home, and glad relief,
And plied the beverage from his own fair sheaf,
That fired his Highland blood with mickle glee;
And England sent her men, of men the chief,
Who taught those sires of Empire yet to be,
To plant the tree of life, to plant fair Freedom's tree!

VII.

Here was not mingled in the city's pomp
Of life's extremes the grandeur and the gloom :
Judgment awoke not here her dismal tromp,
Nor seal'd in blood a fellow-creature's doom,
Nor mourned the captive in a living tomb.
One venerable man, beloved of all,
Sufficed where innocence was yet in bloom,
To sway the strife, that seldom might befal ;
And Albert was their judge in patriarchal hall.

VIII.

How rev'rend was the look, serenely aged,
He bore, this gentle Pennsylvanian sire,
Where all but kindly fervours were assuaged,
Undimm'd by weakness' shade, or turbid ire !
And though amidst the calm of thought entire,
Some high and haughty features might betray
A soul impetuous once, 'twas earthly fire
That fled composure's intellectual ray,
As Ætna's fires grow dim before the rising day.

IX.

I boast no song in magic wonders rife,
But yet familiar, is there nought to prize,
Oh, Nature ! in thy bosom-scenes of life ?
And dwells in daylight truth's salubrious skies
No form with which the soul may sympathise ?
Young, innocent, on whose sweet forehead mild
The parted ringlet shone in simplest guise,
An inmate in the home of Albert smiled,
Or blest his noonday walk—she was his only child.

X.

The rose of England bloom'd on Gertrude's cheek—
What though these shades had seen her birth, her sire
A Briton's independence taught to seek
Far western worlds ; and there his household fire
The light of social love did long inspire,
And many a halcyon day he lived to see
Unbroken, but by one misfortune dire,
When fate had reft his mutual heart—but she
Was gone—and Gertrude climb'd a widow'd father's knee ;

XI.

A loved bequest, and I may half impart
To them that feel the strong paternal tie,
How like a new existence to his heart
Uprose that living flower beneath his eye,
Dear as she was, from cherub infancy,
From hours when she would round his garden play,
To time when, as the ripening years went by,
Her lovely mind could culture well repay,
And more engaging grew from pleasing day to day.

XII.

I may not paint those thousand infant charms ;
(Unconscious fascination, undesign'd !)
The orison repeated in his arms,
For God to bless her sire and all mankind ;
The book, the bosom on his knee reclined,
Or how sweet fairy-lore he heard her con
(The playmate ere the teacher of her mind) :
All uncompanion'd else her years had gone
Till now in Gertrude's eyes their ninth blue summer shone.

XIII.

And summer was the tide, and sweet the hour
When sire and daughter saw, with fleet descent,
An Indian from his bark approach their bower,
Of buskin'd limb, and swarthy lineament!

The red wild feathers on his brow were blent,
And bracelets bound the arm that help'd to light
A boy, who seem'd, as he beside him went,
Of Christian vesture, and complexion bright,
Led by his dusky guide like morning brought by night.

XIV.

Yet pensive seem'd the boy for one so young,
The dimple from his polish'd cheek had fled ;
When, leaning on his forest-bow unstrung,
Th' Oneyda warrior to the planter said,
And laid his hand upon the stripling's head,
" Peace be to thee ! my words this belt approve ;[5]
The paths of peace my steps have hither led :[6]
This little nursling, take him to thy love,
And shield the bird unfledged, since gone the parent dove.

XV.

" Christian ! I am the foeman of thy foe ;
Our wampum league thy brethren did embrace :

Upon the Michigan, three moons ago,
We launch'd our quivers for the bison chase ;
And with the Hurons planted for a space,
With true and faithful hands, the olive-stalk ;

But snakes are in the bosoms of their race,
And though they held with us a friendly talk,
The hollow peace-tree fell beneath their tomahawk!

XVI.

"It was encamping on the lake's far port,
A cry of Areouski[7] broke our sleep,
Where storm'd an ambush'd foe thy nation's fort,
And rapid, rapid whoops came o'er the deep;
But long thy country's war-sign on the steep
Appear'd through ghastly intervals of light,
And deathfully their thunders seem'd to sweep,
Till utter darkness swallow'd up the sight,
As if a shower of blood had quench'd the fiery fight!

XVII.

"It slept—it rose again—on high their tower
Sprung upwards like a torch to light the skies,
Then down again it rain'd an ember shower,
And louder lamentations heard we rise;

As when the evil Manitou[8] that dries
Th' Ohio woods, consumes them in his ire,

In vain the desolated panther flies,
And howls amidst his wilderness of fire :
Alas ! too late we reach'd and smote those Hurons dire !

XVIII.

" But as the fox beneath the nobler hound,
So died their warriors by our battle-brand ;
And from the tree we with her child unbound
A lonely mother of the Christian land—
Her lord—the captain of the British band—
Amidst the slaughter of his soldiers lay ;
Scarce knew the widow our deliv'ring hand ;
Upon her child she sobb'd, and swoon'd away ;
Or shriek'd unto the God to whom the Christians pray.—

XIX.

" Our virgins fed her with their kindly bowls
Of fever-balm, and sweet sagamité ;[9]
But she was journeying to the land of souls,
And lifted up her dying head to pray

That we should bid an ancient friend convey
Her orphan to his home of England's shore ;
And take, she said, this token far away
To one that will remember us of yore,
When he beholds the ring that Waldegrave's Julia wore.—



D

XX.

" And I, the eagle of my tribe, have rush'd
With this lorn dove."[10]—A sage's self-command
Had quell'd the tears from Albert's heart that gush'd ;
But yet his cheek—his agitated hand—
That shower'd upon the stranger of the land
No common boon, in grief but ill beguiled
A soul that was not wont to be unmann'd ;
" And stay," he cried, " dear pilgrim of the wild !
Preserver of my old, my boon companion's child !—

XXI.

" Child of a race whose name my bosom warms
On earth's remotest bounds, how welcome here !
Whose mother oft, a child, has fill'd these arms,
Young as thyself, and innocently dear :
Whose grandsire was my early life's compeer :
Ah, happiest home of England's happy clime !
How beautiful e'en now thy scenes appear,
As in the noon and sunshine of my prime !
How gone, like yesterday, these thrice ten years of time !

XXII.

"And, Julia! when thou wert like Gertrude now,
Can I forget thee, fav'rite child of yore?
Or thought I, in thy father's house when thou
Wert lightest hearted on his festive floor,
And first of all his hospitable door,
To meet and kiss me at my journey's end!
But where was I when Waldegrave was no more?
And thou didst, pale, thy gentle head extend,
In woes, that e'en the tribe of deserts was thy friend!"

XXIII.

He said—and strain'd unto his heart the boy:
Far differently the mute Oneyda took
His calumet of peace,[11] and cup of joy;
As monumental bronze unchanged his look:
A soul that pity touch'd, but never shook:
Train'd, from his tree-rock'd cradle to his bier,[12]
The fierce extremes of good and ill to brook
Impassive—fearing but the shame of fear—
A stoic of the woods—a man without a tear.—

XXIV.

Yet deem not goodness on the savage stock
Of Outalissi's heart disdain'd to grow;
As lives the oak unwither'd on the rock
By storms above, and barrenness below:
He scorn'd his own, who felt another's woe:
And ere the wolf-skin on his back he flung,
Or laced his moccasins,[13] in act to go,
A song of parting to the boy he sung,
Who slept on Albert's couch, nor heard his friendly tongue.

XXV.

"Sleep, wearied one! and in the dreaming land
Shouldst thou the spirit of thy mother greet,
Oh! say, to-morrow, that the white man's hand
Hath pluck'd the thorns of sorrow from thy feet;
While I in lonely wilderness shall meet
Thy little foot-prints—or by traces know
The fountain, where at noon I thought it sweet
To feed thee with the quarry of my bow,
And pour'd the lotus-horn,[14] or slew the mountain roe.

XXVI.

"Adieu! sweet scion of the rising sun!
But should affliction's storms thy blossom mock,
Then come again—my own adopted one!
And I will graft thee on a noble stock:

The crocodile, the condor of the rock,
Shall be the pastime of thy sylvan wars;
And I will teach thee, in the battle's shock,
To pay with Huron blood thy father's scars,
And gratulate his soul rejoicing in the stars!"—

XXVII.

So finish'd he the rhyme (howe'er uncouth)
That true to nature's fervid feelings ran;
(And song is but the eloquence of truth:)
Then forth uprose that lone wayfaring man;[15]
But dauntless he, nor chart, nor journey's plan
In woods required, whose trainèd eye was keen
As eagle of the wilderness, to scan
His path, by mountain, swamp, or deep ravine,
Or ken far friendly huts on good savannahs green.

XXVIII.

Old Albert saw him from the valley's side—
His pirogue launch'd—his pilgrimage begun—

Far, like the red-bird's wing, he seem'd to glide ;
Then dived, and vanish'd in the woodlands dun.
Oft to that spot by tender memory won,
Would Albert climb the promontory's height,

If but a dim sail glimmer'd in the sun ;
But never more, to bless his longing sight,
Was Outalissi hail'd, his bark and plumage bright.

PART II.

A VALLEY from the river shore withdrawn
Was Albert's home, two quiet woods between,

Whose lofty verdure overlook'd his lawn ;
And waters to their resting-place serene
Came fresh'ning, and reflecting all the scene :
(A mirror in the depth of flowery shelves :)
So sweet a spot of earth you might (I ween)
Have guess'd some congregation of the elves,
To sport by summer moons, had shaped it for themselves.

II.

Yet wanted not the eye far scope to muse,
Nor vistas open'd by the wand'ring stream ;
Both where at evening Alleghany views,
Through ridges burning in her western beam,
Lake after lake interminably gleam :
And past those settlers' haunts the eye might roam,
Where earth's unliving silence all would seem ;
Save where on rocks the beaver built his dome,
Or buffalo remote low'd far from human home.

III.

But silent not that adverse eastern path
Which saw Aurora's hills th' horizon crown ;
There was the river heard, in bed of wrath,
(A precipice of foam from mountains brown,)
Like tumults heard from some far-distant town ;
But soft'ning in approach he left his gloom,
And murmur'd pleasantly, and laid him down,
To kiss those easy curving banks of bloom,
That lent the windward air an exquisite perfume.

IV.

It seem'd as if those scenes sweet influence had
On Gertrude's soul, and kindness like their own
Inspired those eyes affectionate and glad,
That seem'd to love whate'er they look'd upon ;
Whether with Hebe's mirth her features shone,
Or if a shade more pleasing them o'ercast,
(As if for heav'nly musing meant alone,)
Yet so becomingly th' expression past,
That each succeeding look was lovelier than the last.

V.

Nor, guess I, was that Pennsylvanian home,
With all its picturesque and balmy grace,
And fields that were a luxury to roam,
Lost on the soul that look'd from such a face !
Enthusiast of the woods ! when years apace
Had bound thy lovely waist with woman's zone,
The sunrise path, at morn, I see thee trace
To hills with high magnolia overgrown ;
And joy to breathe the groves, romantic and alone.

VI.

The sunrise drew her thoughts to Europe forth,
That thus apostrophized its viewless scene :
" Land of my father's love, my mother's birth !
The home of kindred I have never seen !
We know not other—oceans are between ;
Yet, say ! far friendly hearts from whence we came,
Of us does oft remembrance intervene ?
My mother, sure—my sire a thought may claim ;
But Gertrude is to you an unregarded name.

VII.

"And yet, loved England! when thy name I trace
In many a pilgrim's tale and poet's song,
How can I choose but wish for one embrace
Of them, the dear unknown, to whom belong
My mother's looks,—perhaps her likeness strong?

Oh, parent! with what reverential awe,
From features of thine own related throng,
An image of thy face my soul could draw!
And see thee once again whom I too shortly saw!"

VIII.

Yet deem not Gertrude sigh'd for foreign joy;
To soothe a father's couch her only care,
And keep his rev'rend head from all annoy:
For this, methinks, her homeward steps repair,
Soon as the morning wreath had bound her hair:
While yet the wild deer trod in spangling dew,
While boatman caroll'd to the fresh-blown air,
And woods a horizontal shadow threw,
And early fox appear'd in momentary view.—

IX.

At times there was a deep untrodden grot,
Where oft the reading hours sweet Gertrude wore;
Tradition had not named its lonely spot;
But here (methinks) might India's sons explore

Their father's dust,[1] or lift, perchance, of yore,
Their voice to the Great Spirit :—rocks sublime

To human art a sportive semblance wore ;
And yellow lichens colour'd all the clime,
Like moonlit battlements, and tow'rs decay'd by time.

X.

But high, in amphitheatre above,
His arms the everlasting aloe threw :
Breathed but an air of heav'n, and all the grove
As if with instinct living spirit grew,
Rolling its verdant gulfs of every hue ;
And now suspended was the pleasing din,
Now from a murmur faint it swell'd anew,
Like the first note of organ heard within
Cathedral aisles,—ere yet its symphony begin.

XI.

It was in this lone valley she would charm
The ling'ring noon, where flow'rs a couch had strown ;
Her cheek reclining, and her snowy arm
On hillock by the palm-tree half o'ergrown :
And aye that volume on her lap is thrown,

Which every heart of human mould endears;
With Shakspeare's self she speaks and smiles alone,
And no intruding visitation fears,
To shame th' unconscious laugh, or stop her sweetest tears.—

XII.

For, save her presence, scarce an ear had heard
The stock-dove plaining through its gloom profound,
Or winglet of the fairy humming-bird,
Like atoms of the rainbow fluttering round ;
Till chance had usher'd to its inmost ground
The stranger guest of many a distant clime ;
He was, to weet, for eastern mountains bound ;
But late th' equator suns his cheek had tann'd,
And California's gales his roving bosom fann'd.

XIII.

A steed, whose rein hung loosely o'er his arm,
He led dismounted ; ere his leisure pace,
Amid the brown leaves, could her ear alarm,
Close he had come, and worshipp'd for a space
Those downcast features :—she her lovely face
Uplift on one whose lineaments and frame
Were youth and manhood's intermingled grace :
Iberian seem'd his boot—his robe the same,
And well the Spanish plume his lofty looks became.

For Albert's home he sought—her finger fair
Has pointed where the father's mansion stood.

Returning from the copse he soon was there,
And soon as Gertrude hied from dark-green wood ;
Nor joyless, by the converse, understood,
Between the man of age and pilgrim young,
That gay congeniality of mood,
And early liking from acquaintance sprung :
Full fluently conversed their guest in England's tongue.

XV.

And well could he his pilgrimage of taste
Unfold,—and much they loved his fervid strain,—
While he each fair variety retraced
Of climes, and manners, o'er the eastern main :—
Now happy Switzer's hills—romantic Spain—
Gay lilied fields of France—or, more refined,
The soft Ausonia's monumental reign ;
Nor less each rural image he design'd,
Than all the city's pomp and home of human kind.

XVI.

Anon some wilder portraiture he draws ;
Of Nature's savage glories he would speak,—
The loneliness of earth that overawes,—

Where, resting by some tomb of old Cacique,
The lama-driver on Peruvia's peak,

Nor voice nor living motion marks around;
But storks that to the boundless forest shriek;
Or wild-cane arch high flung o'er gulf profound,[2]
That fluctuates when the storms of El Dorado sound.

XVII.

Pleased with his guest, the good man still would ply
Each earnest question, and his converse court;
But Gertrude, as she eyed him, knew not why
A strange and troubling wonder stopt her short.
"In England thou hast been,—and, by report,
An orphan's name (quoth Albert) mayst have known:
Sad tale!—when latest fell our frontier fort,
One innocent—one soldier's child—alone
Was spared, and brought to me, who loved him as my own.—

XVIII.

"Young Henry Waldegrave! three delightful years
These very walls his infant sports did see;
But most I loved him when his parting tears
Alternately bedew'd my child and me:

His sorest parting, Gertrude, was from thee ;
Nor half its grief his little heart could hold :
By kindred he was sent for o'er the sea ;
They tore him from us when but twelve years old,
And scarcely for his loss have I been yet consoled."—

XIX.

His face the wand'rer hid ; but could not hide
A tear, a smile, upon his cheek that dwell ;—
" And speak, mysterious stranger !" Gertrude cried ;
" It is !—it is !—I knew—I knew him well !
'Tis Waldegrave's self, of Waldegrave come to tell !"
A burst of joy the father's lips declare ;
But Gertrude speechless on his bosom fell !
At once his open arms embraced the pair—
Was never group more blest, in this wide world of care.

XX.

" And will ye pardon, then," replied the youth,
" Your Waldegrave's feign'd name, and false attire ?
I durst not in the neighbourhood, in truth,
The very fortunes of your house inquire :
Lest one that knew me might some tidings dire
Impart, and I my weakness all betray ;
For had I lost my Gertrude, and my sire,
I meant but o'er your tombs to weep a day :
Unknown I meant to weep, unknown to pass away.

"But here ye live,—ye bloom,—in each dear face
The changing hand of time I may not blame;

For there, it hath but shed more reverend grace,
And here, of beauty perfected the frame ;
And well I know your hearts are still the same ;
They could not change—ye look the very way,
As when an orphan first to you I came.
And have ye heard of my poor guide, I pray ?
Nay, wherefore weep we, friends, on such a joyous day ?"—

XXII.

"And art thou here ? or is it but a dream ?
And wilt thou, Waldegrave, wilt thou leave us more ?"
"No, never ! thou that yet dost lovelier seem
Than aught on earth—than e'en thyself of yore—
I will not part thee from thy father's shore ;
But we shall cherish him with mutual arms ;
And hand in hand again the path explore,
Which every ray of young remembrance warms ;
While thou shalt be my own with all thy truth and charms."

XXIII.

At morn, as if beneath a galaxy
Of overarching groves in blossoms white,
Where all was od'rous scent and harmony,

And gladness to the heart, nerve, ear, and sight :
There, if, oh gentle love ! I read aright,
The utterance that seal'd thy sacred bond,
'Twas list'ning to these accents of delight,
She hid upon his breast those eyes, beyond
Expression's pow'r to paint, all languishingly fond.

XXIV.

" Flow'r of my life, so lovely and so lone !
Whom I would rather in this desert meet,
Scorning and scorn'd by fortune's pow'r, than own
Her pomp and splendours lavish'd at my feet !
Turn not from me thy breath, more exquisite
Than odours cast on heaven's own shrine—to please—
Give me thy love, than luxury more sweet,
And more than all the wealth that loads the breeze,
When Coromandel's ships return from Indian seas."—

XXV.

Then would that home admit them—happier far
Than grandeur's most magnificent saloon—
While, here and there, a solitary star
Flush'd in the dark'ning firmament of June ;

And silence brought the soul-felt hour full soon,
Ineffable, which I may not portray ;
For never did the Hymenean moon
A paradise of hearts more sacred sway,
In all that slept beneath her soft voluptuous ray.

PART III

O Love! in such a wilderness as this,
Where transport and security entwine,

Here is the empire of thy perfect bliss,
And here thou art a god indeed divine.
Here shall no forms abridge, no hours confine
The views, the walks, that boundless joy inspire!
Roll on, ye days of raptured influence, shine!
Nor, blind with ecstasy's celestial fire,
Shall love behold the spark of earth-born time expire.

II.

Three little moons, how short, amidst the grove
And pastoral savannahs, they consume!
While she, beside her buskin'd youth to rove,
Delights, in fancifully wild costume,
Her lovely brow to shade with Indian plume;
And forth in hunter-seeming vest they fare;
But not to chase the deer in forest gloom;
'Tis but the breath of heav'n—the blessed air—
And interchange of hearts unknown, unseen to share.

III.

What though the sportive dog oft round them note,
Or fawn, or wild bird bursting on the wing;
Yet who, in love's own presence, would devote

To death those gentle throats that wake the spring ;
Or writhing from the brook its victim bring ?
No !—nor let fear one little warbler rouse ;
But, fed by Gertrude's hand, still let them sing,
Acquaintance of her path, amidst the boughs,
That shade e'en now her love, and witness'd first her vows.

IV.

Now labyrinths, which but themselves can pierce,
Methinks, conduct them to some pleasant ground,
Where welcome hills shut out the universe,
And pines their lawny walk encompass round ;
There, if a pause delicious converse found,
'Twas but when o'er each heart th' idea stole,
(Perchance awhile in joy's oblivion drown'd,)
That come what may, while life's glad pulses roll,
Indissolubly thus should soul be knit to soul.

V.

And in the visions of romantic youth,
What years of endless bliss are yet to flow !
But mortal pleasure, what art thou in truth ?
The torrent's smoothness ere it dash below !
And must I change my song ? and must I show,
Sweet Wyoming ! the day, when thou wert doom'd,
Guiltless, to mourn thy loveliest bow'rs laid low ?
When where of yesterday a garden bloom'd,
Death overspread his pall, and black'ning ashes gloom'd !

VI.

Sad was the year, by proud oppression driv'n,
When Transatlantic Liberty arose,
Not in the sunshine, and the smile of heav'n,
But wrapt in whirlwinds, and begirt with woes,

Amidst the strife of fratricidal foes,
Her birth-star was the light of burning plains ;[1]
Her baptism is the weight of blood that flows
From kindred hearts—the blood of British veins—
And famine tracks her steps, and pestilential pains.

VII.

Yet, ere the storm of death had raged remote,
Or siege unseen in heav'n reflects its beams,
Who now each dreadful circumstance shall note,
That fills pale Gertrude's thoughts and nightly dreams !
Dismal to her the forge of battle gleams,
Portentous light ! and music's voice is dumb ;
Save where the fife its shrill reveillé screams,
Or midnight streets re-echo to the drum,
That speaks of madd'ning strife, and blood-stain'd fields to come.

VIII.

It was in truth a momentary pang ;
Yet how comprising myriad shapes of woe !
First when in Gertrude's ear the summons rang,
A husband to the battle doom'd to go !

" Nay meet not thou," she cried, " thy kindred foe !
But peaceful let us seek fair England's strand !"
" Ah, Gertrude ! thy beloved heart, I know,
Would feel, like mine, the stigmatizing brand,
Could I forsake the cause of Freedom's holy band !

IX.

"But shame—but flight—a recreant's name to prove,
To hide in exile ignominious fears;
Say, e'en if this I brook'd, the public love
Thy father's bosom to his home endears:
And how could I his few remaining years,
My Gertrude, sever from so dear a child?"
So, day by day, her boding heart he cheers:
At last that heart to hope is half beguiled,—
And pale through tears suppress'd the mournful beauty smiled.

X.

Night came,—and in their lighted bow'r full late
The joy of converse had endured,—when, hark!
Abrupt and loud, a summons shook their gate:
And, heedless of the dog's obstrep'rous bark,
A form has rush'd amidst them from the dark,
And spread his arms,—and fell upon the floor;
Of aged strength his limbs retain'd the mark;
But desolate he look'd, and famish'd, poor,
As ever shipwreck'd wretch lone left on desert shore.

XI.

Uprisen, each wond'ring brow is knit and arch'd :
A spirit from the dead they deem him first :
To speak he tries ; but quivering, pale, and parch'd,
From lips, as by some pow'rless dream accursed,

Emotions unintelligible burst;
And long his filmed eye is red and dim;
At length the pity-proffer'd cup his thirst
Had half assuaged, and nerved his shuddering limb,
When Albert's hand he grasp'd;—but Albert knew not him.

XII.

"And hast thou, then, forgot," (he cried, forlorn,
And eyed the group with half indignant air,)
"Oh! hast thou, Christian chief, forgot the morn
When I with thee the cup of peace did share?
Then stately was this head, and dark this hair,
That now is white as Appalachia's snow;
But, if the weight of fifteen years' despair
And age hath bow'd me, and the tort'ring foe,
Bring me my boy—and he will his deliverer know!"

XIII.

It was not long, with eyes and heart of flame,
Ere Henry to his loved Oneyda flew:
"Bless thee, my guide!"—but backward, as he came,
The chief his old bewilder'd head withdrew,

And grasp'd his arm, and look'd, and look'd him through.
'Twas strange—nor could the group a smile control—
The long, the doubtful scrutiny to view:

At last, delight o'er all his features stole,
"It is—my own," he cried, and clasp'd him to his soul.

XIV.

"Yes! thou recall'st my pride of years, for then
The bowstring of my spirit was not slack,
When, spite of woods, and floods, and ambush'd men,
I bore thee like the quiver on my back,
Fleet as the whirlwind hurries on the rack;
Nor foeman then, nor cougar's[2] crouch I fear'd,
For I was strong as mountain cataract:
And dost thou not remember how we cheer'd
Upon the last hill-top, when white men's huts appear'd!

XV.

"Then welcome be my death-song, and my death!
Since I have seen thee, and again embraced."
And longer had he spent his toil-worn breath;
But, with affectionate and eager haste,
Was every arm outstretch'd around their guest,
To welcome and to bless his aged head.
Soon was the hospitable banquet placed;

And Gertrude's lovely hands a balsam shed

On wounds with fever'd joy that more profusely bled.

XVI.

" But this is not a time,"—he started up,
And smote his breast with woe-denouncing hand—
" This is no time to fill the joyous cup,
The Mammoth comes,[3]—the foe,—the Monster Brandt,—
With all his howling desolating band ;—
These eyes have seen their blade and burning pine
Awake at once, and silence half your land.
Red is the cup they drink ; but not with wine :
Awake, and watch to-night, or see no morning shine !

XVII.

" Scorning to wield the hatchet for his bribe,
'Gainst Brandt himself I went to battle forth :[4]
Accursed Brandt ! he left of all my tribe
Nor man, nor child, nor thing of living birth :
No ! not the dog that watch'd my household hearth
Escaped that night of blood, upon our plains !
All perish'd !—I alone am left on earth !
To whom nor relative nor blood remains ;
No !—not a kindred drop that runs in human veins ![5]

XVIII.

"But go !—and rouse your warriors ;—for, if right
These old bewilder'd eyes could guess, by signs
Of striped and starred banners, on yon height
Of eastern cedars, o'er the creek of pines—
Some fort embattled by your country shines :
Deep roars the innavigable gulf below
Its squared rocks, and palisaded lines.
Go ! seek the light its warlike beacons show ;
Whilst I in ambush wait, for vengeance, and the foe !"

XIX.

Scarce had he utter'd,—when heav'n's verge extreme
Reverberates the bomb's descending star,—
And sounds that mingled laugh,—and shout,—and scream,
To freeze the blood, in one discordant jar,
Rung to the pealing thunderbolts of war.
Whoop after whoop with rack the ear assail'd,
As if unearthly fiends had burst their bar ;
While rapidly the marksman's shot prevail'd ;—
And ay, as if for death, some lonely trumpet wail'd.—

XX.

Then look'd they to the hills, where fire o'erhung
The bandit groups, in one Vesuvian glare ;
Or swept, far seen, the tow'r, whose clock unrung,
Told legible that midnight of despair.
She faints,—she falters not,—th' heroic fair,—
As he the sword and plume in haste array'd.
One short embrace—he clasp'd his dearest care—
But hark ! what nearer war-drum shakes the glade ?
Joy, joy ! Columbia's friends are trampling through the shade !

XXI.

Then came of every race the mingled swarm,
Far rung the groves, and gleam'd the midnight grass,
With flambeau, javelin, and naked arm ;
As warriors wheel'd their culverins of brass,
Sprung from the woods, a bold athletic mass,
Whom virtue fires, and liberty combines :
And first the wild Moravian yagers pass ;
His plumed host the dark Iberian joins—
And Scotia's sword beneath the Highland thistle shines.

XXII.

And in—the buskin'd hunters of the deer,
To Albert's home with shout and cymbal throng :—
Roused by their warlike pomp, and mirth and cheer,
Old Outalissi woke his battle song,

And, beating with his war-club cadence strong,
Tells how his deep-stung indignation smarts,
Of them that wrapt his house in flames, ere long,
To whet a dagger on their stony hearts,
And smile avenged ere yet his eagle spirit parts.

XXIII.

Calm, opposite the Christian father rose,
Pale on his venerable brow its rays
Of martyr light the conflagration throws ;
One hand upon his lovely child he lays,
And one th' uncover'd crowd to silence sways ,
While, though the battle flash is faster driv'n,—
Unawed, with eye unstartled by the blaze,
He for his bleeding country prays to Heav'n,—
Prays that the men of blood themselves may be forgiven.

XXIV.

Short time is now for gratulating speech ;
And yet, beloved Gertrude, ere began
Thy country's flight, yon distant tow'rs to reach,
Look'd not on thee the rudest partisan

With brow relax'd to love ? And murmurs ran,

As round and round their willing ranks they drew,

From beauty's sight to shield the hostile van.
Grateful, on them a placid look she threw,
Nor wept, but as she bade her mother's grave adieu !

XXV.

Past was the flight, and welcome seem'd the tow'r,
That, like a giant standard-bearer, frown'd
Defiance on the roving Indian pow'r.
Beneath, each bold and promontory mound
With embrasure emboss'd, and armour crown'd,
And arrowy frieze, and wedged ravelin,
Wove like a diadem its tracery round
The lofty summit of that mountain green ;
Here stood secure the group, and eyed a distant scene :

XXVI.

A scene of death ! where fires beneath the sun,
And blended arms, and white pavilions glow ;
And for the business of destruction done,
Its requiem the war-horn seem'd to blow.

There, sad spectatress of her country's woe!
The lovely Gertrude, safe from present harm,
Had laid her cheek, and clasp'd her hands of snow
On Waldegrave's shoulder, half within his arm
Enclosed, that felt her heart, and hush'd its wild alarm!

XXVII.

But short that contemplation—sad and short
The pause to bid each much-loved scene adieu!
Beneath the very shadow of the fort,
Where friendly swords were drawn, and banners flew!
Ah! who could deem that foot of Indian crew
Was near?—yet there, with lust of murd'rous deeds,
Gleam'd like a basilisk, from woods in view,
The ambush'd foeman's eye—his volley speeds,
And Albert—Albert falls! the dear old father bleeds!

XXVIII.

And tranced in giddy horror, Gertrude swoon'd;
Yet, while she clasps him lifeless to her zone,
Say, burst they, borrow'd from her father's wound,
These drops?—Oh God! the life-blood is her own;
And, falt'ring, on her Waldegrave's bosom thrown—
"Weep not, O love!" she cries, "to see me bleed—
Thee, Gertrude's sad survivor, thee alone—
Heaven's peace commiserate; for scarce I heed
These wounds:—yet thee to leave is death, is death indeed.

"Clasp me a little longer, on the brink
Of fate! while I can feel thy dear caress;

And, when this heart hath ceased to beat—oh! think,
And let it mitigate thy woe's excess,
That thou hast been to me all tenderness,
And friend to more than human friendship just.
Oh! by that retrospect of happiness,
And by the hopes of an immortal trust,
God shall assuage thy pangs—when I am laid in dust!

XXX.

"Go, Henry, go not back, when I depart,
The scene thy bursting tears too deep will move,
Where my dear father took thee to his heart,
And Gertrude thought it ecstasy to rove
With thee, as with an angel, through the grove
Of peace,—imagining her lot was cast
In heav'n; for ours was not like earthly love.
And must this parting be our very last?
No! I shall love thee still, when death itself is past.

XXXI.

"Half could I bear, methinks, to leave this earth,—
And thee, more loved than aught beneath the sun,

If I had lived to smile but on the birth
Of one dear pledge ;—but shall there, then, be none,
In future times—no gentle little one,
To clasp thy neck, and look, resembling me ?
Yet seems it, e'en while life's last pulses run,
A sweetness in the cup of death to be,
Lord of my bosom's love ! to die beholding thee !"

XXXII.

Hush'd were his Gertrude's lips ; but still their bland
And beautiful expression seem'd to melt
With love that could not die ! and still his hand
She presses to the heart no more that felt.
Ah heart ! where once each fond affection dwelt,
And features yet that spoke a soul more fair.
Mute, gazing, agonizing as he knelt,—
Of them that stood encircling his despair,
He heard some friendly words ;—but knew not what they
were.

XXXIII.

For now, to mourn their judge and child, arrives
A faithful band. With solemn rites between,

'Twas sung, how they were lovely in their lives,
And in their deaths had not divided been.
Touch'd by the music, and the melting scene,
Was scarce one tearless eye amidst the crowd :—
Stern warriors, resting on their swords, were seen
To veil their eyes, as pass'd each much-loved shroud—
While woman's softer soul in woe dissolved aloud.

XXXIV.

Then mournfully the parting bugle bid
Its farewell o'er the grave of worth and truth ;
Prone to the dust, afflicted Waldegrave hid
His face on earth ;—him watch'd in gloomy ruth,
His woodland guide ; but words had none to soothe
The grief that knew not consolation's name !
Casting his Indian mantle o'er the youth,
He watch'd, beneath its folds, each burst that came
Convulsive, ague-like, across his shuddering frame !

XXXV.

"And I could weep ;"—th' Oneyda chief
His descant wildly thus began :

"But that I may not stain with grief
The death-song of my father's son!
Or bow this head in woe;
For by my wrongs, and by my wrath!
To-morrow Areouski's breath
(That fires yon heav'n with storms of death)

Shall light us to the foe :
And we shall share, my Christian boy !
The foeman's blood, the avenger's joy !—

XXXVI.

" But thee, my flow'r, whose breath was giv'n
By milder genii o'er the deep,
The spirits of the white man's heav'n
Forbid not thee to weep :—
Nor will the Christian host,
Nor will thy father's spirit grieve
To see thee, on the battle's eve,
Lamenting take a mournful leave
Of her who loved thee most :
She was the rainbow to thy sight !
Thy sun—thy heav'n—of lost delight !—

XXXVII.

" To-morrow let us do or die !
But when the bolt of death is hurl'd,
Ah ! whither then with thee to fly,
Shall Outalissi roam the world ?
Seek we thy once-loved home ?—
The hand is gone that cropt its flowers !

Unheard their clock repeats its hours!—
Cold is the hearth within their bow'rs!—
And should we thither roam,
Its echoes, and its empty tread,
Would sound like voices from the dead!

XXXVIII.

"Or shall we cross yon mountains blue,
Whose streams my kindred nation quaff'd;
And by my side, in battle true,
A thousand warriors drew the shaft?
Ah! there in desolation cold,
The desert serpent dwells alone,
Where grass o'ergrows each mould'ring bone,
And stones themselves to ruin grown,
Like me, are death-like old.
Then seek we not their camp—for there—
The silence dwells of my despair!

XXXIX.

"But hark, the trump!—to-morrow thou
In glory's fire shalt dry thy tears:
E'en from the land of shadows now
My father's awful ghost appears;

Amidst the clouds that round us roll,
He bids my soul for battle thirst—
He bids me dry the last—the first—
The only tears that ever burst—
From Outalissi's soul ;
Because I may not stain with grief
The death-song of an Indian chief."

# NOTES.

# NOTES.

## PART I.

[1] P. 6. *From merry mock-bird's song.*]—The mocking-bird is of the form of, but larger, than the thrush; and the colours are a mixture of black, white, and grey. What is said of the nightingale, by its greatest admirers, is what may with more propriety apply to this bird, who, in a natural state, sings with very superior taste. Towards evening I have heard one begin softly, reserving its breath to swell certain notes, which, by this means, had a most astonishing effect. A gentleman in London had one of these birds for six years. During the space of a minute he was heard to imitate the wood-lark, chaffinch, blackbird, thrush, and sparrow. In this country (America) I have frequently known the mocking-birds so engaged in this mimicry, that it was with much difficulty I could ever obtain an opportunity of hearing their own natural note. Some go so far as to say, that they have neither peculiar notes, nor favourite imitations. This may be denied. Their few natural notes resemble those of the (European) nightingale. Their song, however, has a greater compass and volume than the nightingale's, and they have the faculty of varying all intermediate notes in a manner which is truly delightful.—*Ashe's Travels in America,* vol. ii. p. 73.

[2] P. 7. *Green Albyn.*]—Scotland.

[3] P. 7. *Thy pellochs.*]—Pelloch is the Gaelic appellation for porpoise.

[4] P. 7. *And distant isles that hear the loud Corbrechtan roar.*]—The Corybrechtan, or Corbrechtan, is a whirlpool on the western coast of Scotland, near the island of Jura, which is heard at a prodigious distance. Its name signifies the whirlpool of the Prince of Denmark; and there is a tradition that

a Danish Prince once undertook, for a wager, to cast anchor in it. He is said to have used woollen instead of hempen ropes, for greater strength, but perished in the attempt. On the shores of Argyleshire I have often listened with great delight to the sound of this vortex, at the distance of many leagues. When the weather is calm, and the adjacent sea scarcely heard on these picturesque shores, its sound, which is like the sound of innumerable chariots, creates a magnificent and fine effect.

P. 11. *Of buskin'd limb, and swarthy lineament.*]—In the Indian tribes there is a great similarity in their colour, stature, &c. They are all, except the Snake Indians, tall in stature, straight, and robust. It is very seldom they are deformed, which has given rise to the supposition that they put to death their deformed children. Their skin is of a copper colour; their eyes large, bright, black, and sparkling, indicative of a subtle and discerning mind; their hair is of the same colour, and prone to be long, seldom or never curled. Their teeth are large and white; I never observed any decayed among them, which makes their breath as sweet as the air they inhale.—*Travels through America by Captains Lewis and Clarke, in* 1804-5-6.

[5] P. 12. *Peace be to thee! my words this belt approve.*]—The Indians of North America accompany every formal address to strangers, with whom they form or recognise a treaty of amity, with a present of a string, or belt, of wampum. Wampum (says Cadwallader Colden) is made of the large whelk shell, Buccinum, and shaped like long beads: it is the current money of the Indians.—*History of the Five Indian Nations*, p. 34. New York Edition.

[6] P. 12. *The paths of peace my steps have hither led.*]—In relating an interview of Mohawk Indians with the Governor of New York, Colden quotes the following passage as a specimen of their metaphorical manner: "Where shall I seek the chair of peace? Where shall I find it but upon our path? and whither doth our path lead us but unto this house?"

P. 12. *Our wampum league thy brethren did embrace.*]—When they solicit the alliance, offensive or defensive, of a whole nation, they send an embassy with a large belt of wampum and a bloody hatchet, inviting them to come and drink the blood of their enemies. The wampum made use of on these and other occasions, before their acquaintance with the Europeans, was nothing but small shells which they picked up by the sea-coasts, and on the banks of the lakes; and now it is nothing but a kind of cylindrical beads, made of shells, white and black, which are esteemed among them as silver and gold are among us. The black they call the most valuable, and both together are their greatest riches and ornaments; these among them answering all the end that money does amongst us. They have the art of stringing, twisting, and interweaving them into their belts, collars, blankets, moccasins, &c., in ten thousand different sizes, forms, and figures, so as to be ornaments for every part of dress, and expressive to them of all their important transactions. They dye the wampum of various colours and shades, and mix and dispose them with great ingenuity and order, so as to be significant among themselves of almost everything they please; so that by these their words are kept, and their thoughts communicated to one another, as ours are by writing. The belts that pass from one nation to another in all treaties, declarations, and important transactions, are very carefully preserved in the cabins of their chiefs, and serve not only as a kind of record or history, but as a public treasure.—*Major Rogers's Account of North America.*

[7] P. 14. *A cry of Areouski.*]—The Indian God of War.

[8] P. 15. *As when the evil Manitou.*]—It is certain the Indians acknowledge one Supreme Being, or Giver of Life, who presides over all things; that is, the Great Spirit, and they look up to him as the source of good, from whence no evil can proceed. They also believe in a bad Spirit, to whom they ascribe great power; and suppose that through his power all the evils which befal mankind are inflicted. To him, therefore, they pray in their distresses, begging that he would either avert their troubles, or moderate them when they are no longer avoidable.

They hold also that there are good Spirits of a lower degree, who have their particular departments, in which they are constantly contributing to the happiness of mortals. These they suppose to preside over all the extraordinary productions of Nature, such as those lakes, rivers, and mountains that are of an uncommon magnitude; and likewise the beasts, birds, fishes, and even vegetables or stones, that exceed the rest of their species in size or singularity. —*Clarke's Travels among the Indians.*

The Supreme Spirit of Good is called by the Indians, Kitchi Manitou; and the Spirit of Evil, Matchi Manitou.

[9] P. 16. *Of fever-balm, and sweet sagamité.*]—The fever-balm is a medicine used by these tribes; it is a decoction of a bush called the Fever Tree. Sagamité is a kind of soup administered to their sick.

[10] P. 18. *And I, the eagle of my tribe, have rush'd*
*With this lorn dove.*]

The testimony of all travellers among the American Indians who mention their hieroglyphics authorizes me in putting this figurative language in the mouth of Outalissi. The dove is among them, as elsewhere, an emblem of meekness; and the eagle, that of a bold, noble, and liberal mind. When the Indians speak of a warrior who soars above the multitude in person and endowments, they say, "he is like the eagle who destroys his enemies, and gives protection and abundance to the weak of his own tribe."

P. 19. *Far differently the mute Oneyda took, &c.*]—They are extremely circumspect and deliberate in every word and action; nothing hurries them into any intemperate wrath, but that inveteracy to their enemies which is rooted in every Indian's breast. In all other instances they are cool and deliberate, taking care to suppress the emotions of the heart. If an Indian has discovered that a friend of his is in danger of being cut off by a lurking enemy, he does not tell him of his danger in direct terms as though he were in fear, but he first coolly asks him which way he is going that day, and having his answer, with the same indifference tells him that he has been informed that a noxious beast lies on the route he is going. This hint proves sufficient, and his friend avoids the danger with as much caution as though every design and motion of his enemy had been pointed out to him.

If an Indian has been engaged for several days in the chase, and by accident continued long without food, when he arrives at the hut of a friend, where he knows that his wants will be immediately supplied, he takes care not to show the least symptoms of impatience, or betray the extreme hunger that he is tortured with; but on being invited in, sits contentedly down, and smokes his pipe with as much composure as if his appetite was cloyed and he was perfectly at ease. He does the same if among strangers. This custom is strictly adhered to by every tribe, as they esteem it a proof of fortitude, and think the reverse would entitle them to the appellation of old women.

If you tell an Indian that his children have greatly signalised themselves against an enemy, have taken many scalps, and brought home many prisoners, he does not appear to feel any strong emotions of pleasure on the occasion; his answer generally is,—"They have done well," and he makes but very little inquiry about the matter; on the contrary, if you inform him that his children are slain or taken prisoners, he makes no complaints; he only replies, "It is unfortunate:" and for some time asks no questions about how it happened.—*Lewis and Clarke's Travels.*

[11] P. 19. *His calumet of peace, &c.*]—Nor is the calumet of less importance or less revered than the wampum in many transactions relative both to peace and war. The bowl of this pipe is made of a kind of soft red stone, which is easily wrought and hollowed out; the stem is of cane, alder, or some kind of light wood, painted with different colours, and decorated with the heads, tails, and feathers of the most beautiful birds. The use of the calumet is to smoke either tobacco or some bark, leaf, or herb, which they often use instead of it, when they enter into an alliance on any serious occasion, or solemn engagements; this being among them the most sacred oath that can be taken, the violation of which is esteemed most infamous, and deserving of severe punishment from Heaven. When they treat of war, the whole pipe and all its ornaments are red: sometimes it is red only on one side, and by the disposition of the feathers, &c., one acquainted with their customs will know at first sight what the nation who presents it intends or desires. Smoking the calumet is also a religious ceremony on some occasions, and in all treaties is considered as a witness between the parties, or rather as an instrument by which they invoke the sun and moon to witness their sincerity, and to be as it were a guarantee of the treaty between them. This custom of the Indians, though to appearance somewhat ridiculous, is not without its reasons; for as they find that smoking tends to disperse the vapours of the brain, to raise the spirits, and to qualify them for thinking and judging properly, they introduce it into their councils, where, after their resolves, the pipe was considered as a seal of their decrees, and as a pledge of their performance thereof it was sent to those they were consulting, in alliance or treaty with;—so that smoking among them at the same pipe is equivalent to our drinking together and out of the same cup.—*Major Rogers's Account of North America,* 1766.

The lighted calumet is also used among them for a purpose still more interesting than the expression of social friendship. The austere manners of the Indians forbid any appearance of gallantry between the sexes in the day-time; but at night the young lover goes a calumetting, as his courtship is called. As these people live in a state of equality, and without fear of internal violence or theft in their own tribes, they leave their doors open by night as well as by day. The lover takes advantage of this liberty, lights his calumet, enters the cabin of his mistress, and gently presents it to her. If she extinguish it, she admits his addresses; but if she suffer it to burn unnoticed, he retires with a disappointed and throbbing heart.—*Ashe's Travels.*

[12] P. 12. *Train'd, from his tree-rock'd cradle to his bier.*]—An Indian child, as soon as he is born, is swathed with clothes, or skins, and being laid on his

back, is bound down on a piece of thick board, spread over with soft moss. The board is somewhat larger and broader than the child, and bent pieces of wood, like pieces of hoops, are placed over its face to protect it; so that if the machine were suffered to fall, the child probably would not be injured. When the women have any business to transact at home, they hang the boards on a tree, if there be one at hand, and set them a swinging from side to side, like a pendulum, in order to exercise the children.—*Weld*, vol. ii. p. 246.

P. 19. *The fierce extremes of good and ill to brook*
*Impassive*———

Of the active as well as passive fortitude of the Indian character, the following is an instance related by Adair in his Travels:—

"A party of the Senekah Indians came to war against the Katahba, bitter enemies to each other.—In the woods the former discovered a sprightly warrior belonging to the latter, hunting in their usual light dress; on his perceiving them, he sprang off for a hollow rock four or five miles distant, as they intercepted him from running homeward. He was so extremely swift and skilful with the gun, as to kill seven of them in the running fight before they were able to surround and take him. They carried him to their country in sad triumph; but though he had filled them with uncommon grief and shame for the loss of so many of their kindred, yet the love of martial virtue induced them to treat him, during their long journey, with a great deal more civility than if he had acted the part of a coward. The women and children, when they met him at their several towns, beat him and whipped him in as severe a manner as the occasion required, according to their law of justice, and at last he was formally condemned to die by the fiery torture. It might reasonably be imagined that what he had for some time gone through, by being fed with a scanty hand, a tedious march, lying at night on the bare ground, exposed to the changes of the weather, with his arms and legs extended in a pair of rough stocks, and suffering such punishment on his entering into their hostile towns, as a prelude to those sharp torments for which he was destined, would have so impaired his health and affected his imagination, as to have sent him to his long sleep, out of the way of any more sufferings. Probably this would have been the case with the major part of the white people under similar circumstances; but I never knew this with any of the Indians; and this cool-headed, brave warrior did not deviate from their rough lessons of martial virtue, but acted his part so well as to surprise and sorely vex his numerous enemies: for when they were taking him, unpinioned, in their wild parade, to the place of torture, which lay near to a river, he suddenly dashed down those who stood in his way, sprang off, and plunged into the water, swimming underneath like an otter, only rising to take breath, till he reached the opposite shore. He now ascended the steep bank; but though he had good reason to be in a hurry, as many of the enemy were in the water, and others running, very like bloodhounds, in pursuit of him, and the bullets flying around him from the time he took to the river, yet his heart did not allow him to leave them abruptly, without taking leave in a formal manner, in return for the extraordinary favours they had done him, and intended to do him. After slapping a part of his body in defiance to them (continues the author), he put up the shrill war-whoop, as his last salute, till some more convenient opportunity offered, and darted off in the manner of a beast broke loose from its torturing enemies. He continued his speed so as to run by about midnight of the same day as far as his eager pursuers were two days in reaching. There he rested till he happily discovered five of those Indians who had pursued him:—he lay hid a little way off their camp, till they were sound asleep. Every circumstance of his situation occurred to him and inspired him with heroism. He was naked, torn, and hungry, and his enraged enemies were come up with him;—but there was now everything to relieve his wants, and a fair opportunity to save his life, and get great honour and sweet revenge, by cutting them off. Resolution, a convenient spot, and sudden surprise, would effect the main object of all his wishes and hopes. He accordingly crept, took one of their tomahawks, and killed them all on the spot,—clothed himself, took a choice gun, and as much ammunition and provisions as he could well carry in a running march. He set off afresh with a light heart, and did not sleep for several successive nights, only when he reclined, as usual, a little before day, with his back to a tree. As it were by instinct, when he found he was free from the pursuing enemy, he made directly to the very place where he had killed seven of his enemies, and was taken by them for the fiery torture. He digged them up, burnt their bodies to ashes, and went home in safety with singular triumph. Other pursuing enemies came, on the evening of the second day, to the camp of their dead people, when the sight gave them a greater shock than they had ever known before. In their chilled war-council they concluded, that as he had done such surprising things in his defence before he was captivated, and since that in his naked condition, and now was well-armed, if they continued the pursuit he would spoil them all, for he surely was an enemy wizard,—and therefore they returned home."—*Adair's General Observations on the American Indians*, p. 394.

It is surprising (says the same author) to see the long-continued speed of the Indians. Though some of us have often run the swiftest of them out of sight for about the distance of twelve miles, yet afterwards, without any seeming toil, they would stretch on, leave us out of sight, and outwind any horse.—*Ibid.* p. 318.

If an Indian were driven out into the extensive woods, with only a knife and a tomahawk, or a small hatchet, it is not to be doubted but he would fatten even where a wolf would starve. He would soon collect fire by rubbing two dry pieces of wood together, make a bark hut, earthen vessels, and a bow and arrows; then kill wild game, fish, fresh-water tortoises, gather a plentiful variety of vegetables, and live in affluence.—*Ibid.* p. 410.

P. 20. *Or laced his moccasins.*]—Moccasins are a sort of Indian buskins.

P. 20. *Sleep, wearied one! and in the dreaming land*
*Shouldst thou the spirit of thy mother greet.*]

There is nothing (says Charlevoix) in which these barbarians carry their superstitions farther than in what regards dreams; but they vary greatly in their manner of explaining themselves on this point. Sometimes it is the reasonable soul which ranges abroad, while the sensitive continues to animate the body. Sometimes it is the familiar genius who gives salutary counsel with respect to what is going to happen. Sometimes it is a visit made by the soul of the object of which he dreams. But in whatever manner the dream is conceived, it is always looked upon as a thing sacred, and as the most ordinary way in which the gods make known their will to men. Filled with this idea, they cannot conceive how we should pay no regard to them. For the most part they look upon them either as a desire of the soul, inspired by some genius, or an order from him, and in consequence of this principle they hold it a religious duty to obey them. An Indian having dreamt of having a finger cut off, had it really cut off as soon as he awoke, having first prepared himself for this important action by a feast. Another having dreamt of being a prisoner, and in the hands of his enemies, was much at a loss what to do. He consulted the jugglers, and by their advice caused himself to be tied to a post, and burnt in several parts of the body.—*Charlevoix, Journal of a Voyage to North America.*

[14] P. 20. *And pour'd the lotus-horn.*]—From a flower shaped like a horn, which Chateaubriand presumes to be of the lotus kind, the Indians, in their travels through the desert, often find a draught of dew purer than any other water.

P. 22. *The crocodile, the condor of the rock.*]—The alligator, or American crocodile, when full grown (says Bertram), is a very large and terrible creature, and of prodigious strength, activity, and swiftness in the water. I have seen them twenty feet in length, and some are supposed to be twenty-two or twenty-three feet in length. Their body is as large as that of a horse, their shape usually resembles that of a lizard, which is flat, or cuneiform, being compressed on each side, and gradually diminishing from the abdomen to the extremity, which, with the whole body, is covered with horny plates, or squamæ, impenetrable when on the body of the live animal, even to a rifle-ball, except about their head, and just behind their fore-legs or arms, where, it is said, they are only vulnerable. The head of a full-grown one is about three feet, and the mouth opens nearly the same length. Their eyes are small in proportion, and seem sunk in the head, by means of the prominency of the brows; the nostrils are large, inflated, and prominent on the top, so that the head on the water resembles, at a distance, a great chunk of wood floating about: only the upper jaw moves, which they raise almost perpendicular, so as to form a right angle with the lower one. In the forepart of the upper jaw, on each side, just under the nostrils, are two very large, thick, strong teeth, or tusks, not very sharp, but rather the shape of a cone: these are as white as the finest polished ivory, and are not covered by any skin or lips, but always in sight, which gives the creature a frightful appearance: in the lower jaw are holes opposite to these teeth to receive them; when they clap their jaws together, it causes a surprising noise, like that which is made by forcing a heavy plank with violence upon the ground, and may be heard at a great distance. But what is yet more surprising to a stranger, is the incredibly loud and terrifying roar which they are capable of making, especially in breeding-time. It most resembles very heavy distant thunder, not only shaking the air and waters, but causing the earth to tremble; and when hundreds are roaring at the same time, you can scarcely be persuaded but that the whole globe is violently and dangerously agitated. An old champion, who is, perhaps, absolute sovereign of a little lake or lagoon, (when fifty less than himself are obliged to content themselves with swelling and roaring in little coves round about,) darts forth from the reedy coverts, all at once, on the surface of the waters in a right line, at first seemingly as rapid as lightning, but gradually more slowly, until he arrives at the centre of the lake, where he stops. He now swells himself by drawing in wind and water through his mouth, which causes a loud sonorous rattling in the throat for near a minute; but it is immediately forced out again through his mouth and nostrils with a loud noise, brandishing his tail in the air, and the vapour running from his nostrils like smoke. At other times, when swollen to an extent ready to burst, his head and tail lifted up, he spins or twirls round on the surface of the water. He acts his part like an Indian chief, when rehearsing his feats of war.—*Bertram's Travels in North America.*

[15] P. 22. *Then forth uprose that lone wayfaring man.*]—They discover an amazing sagacity, and acquire, with the greatest readiness, anything that depends upon the attention of the mind. By experience, and an acute observation, they attain many perfections to which the Americans are strangers. For instance, they will cross a forest or a plain, which is two hundred miles in breadth, so as to reach with great exactness the point at which they intend to arrive, keeping, during the whole of that space, in a direct line, without any material deviations; and this they will do with the same ease, let the weather be fair or cloudy. With equal acuteness they will point to that part of the heavens the sun is in, though it be intercepted by clouds or fogs. Besides this, they are able to pursue, with incredible facility, the traces of man or beast, either on leaves or grass; and on this account it is with great difficulty they escape discovery. They are indebted for these talents not only to nature, but to an extraordinary command of the intellectual qualities, which can only be acquired by an unremitted attention, and by long experience. They are, in general, very happy in a retentive memory. They can recapitulate every particular that has been treated of in councils, and remember the exact time when they were held. Their belts of wampum preserve the substance of the treaties they have concluded with the neighbouring tribes for ages back, to which they will appeal and refer with as much perspicuity and readiness as Europeans can to their written records.

The Indians are totally unskilled in Geography, as well as all the other sciences, and yet they draw on their birch-bark very exact charts or maps of the countries they are acquainted with. The latitude and longitude only are wanting to make them tolerably complete.

Their sole knowledge in astronomy consists in being able to point out the polar star, by which they regulate their course when they travel in the night.

They reckon the distance of places not by miles or leagues, but by a day's journey, which, according to the best calculation I could make, appears to be about twenty English miles. These they also divide into halves and quarters, and will demonstrate them in their maps with great exactness by the hieroglyphics just mentioned, when they regulate in council their war-parties, or their most distant hunting excursions.—*Lewis and Clarke's Travels.*

Some of the French missionaries have supposed that the Indians are guided by instinct, and have pretended that Indian children can find their way through a forest as easily as a person of maturer years; but this is a most absurd notion. It is unquestionably by a close attention to the growth of the trees, and position of the sun, that they find their way. On the northern side of a tree there is generally the most moss; and the bark on that side, in general, differs from that on the opposite one. The branches toward the south are, for the most part, more luxuriant than those on the other sides of trees, and several other distinctions also subsist between the northern and southern sides, conspicuous to Indians, being taught from their infancy to attend to them; which a common observer would, perhaps, never notice. Being accustomed from their infancy likewise to pay great attention to the position of the sun, they learn to make the most accurate allowance for its apparent motion from one part of the heavens to another; and, in every part of the day, they will point to the part of the heavens where it is, although the sky be obscured by clouds or mists.

An instance of their dexterity in finding their way through an unknown country, came under my observation when I was at Staunton, situated behind the Blue Mountains, Virginia. A number of the Creek nation had arrived at that town on their way to Philadelphia, whither they were going upon some affairs of importance, and had stopped there for the night. In the morning, some circumstance or other, which could not be learned, induced one half of the Indians to set off without their companions, who did not follow until some hours afterwards. When these last were ready to pursue their journey, several of the towns-people mounted their horses to escort them part of the way. They proceeded along the high road for some miles, but, all at once, hastily turning aside into the woods, though there was no path, the Indians advanced confidently forward. The people who accompanied them, surprised at this movement, informed them that they were quitting the road to Philadelphia, and expressed their fear lest they should miss their companions who had gone on before. They answered, that they knew better, that the way through the woods was the shortest to Philadelphia, and that they knew very well that their companions had entered the wood at the very place where they did. Curiosity led some of the horsemen to go on, and, to their astonishment, for there was apparently no track, they overtook the other Indians in the thickest part of the wood. But what appeared most singular was, that the route which they took was found, on examining a map, to be as direct for Philadelphia as if they had taken the bearings by a mariner's compass. From others of their nation, who had been at Philadelphia at a former period, they had probably learned the exact direction of that city from their villages, and had never lost sight of it, although they had already travelled three hundred miles through the woods, and had upwards of four hundred miles more to go before they could reach the place of their destination. Of the exactness with which they can find out a strange place to which they had been once directed by their own people, a striking example is furnished, I think, by Mr. Jefferson, in his account of the Indian graves in Virginia. These graves are nothing more than large mounds of earth in the woods, which, on being opened, are found to contain skeletons in an erect posture: the Indian mode of sepulture has been too often described to remain unknown to you. But to come to my story. A party of Indians that were passing on to some of the sea-ports on the Atlantic, just as the Creeks, above mentioned, were going to Philadelphia, were observed, all on a sudden, to quit the straight road by which they were proceeding, and, without asking any questions, to strike through the woods, in a direct line, to one of these graves, which lay at the distance of some miles from the road. Now very near a century must have passed over since the part of Virginia, in which this grave was situated, had been inhabited by Indians, and these Indian travellers, who were to visit it by themselves, had unquestionably never been in that part of the country before: they must have found their way to it simply from the description of its situation that had been handed down to them by tradition.—*Weld's Travels in North America*, vol. ii.

## PART II.

[1] P. 33. *Their fathers' dust.*]—It is a custom of the Indian tribes to visit the tombs of their ancestors, in the cultivated parts of America, who have been buried for upwards of a century.

[2] P. 40. *Or wild-cane arch high flung o'er gulf profound.*]—The bridges over narrow streams in many parts of Spanish America, are said to be built of cane, which, however strong to support the passenger, are yet waved in the agitation of the storm, and frequently add to the effect of a mountainous and picturesque scenery.

## PART III.

[1] P. 54. *Her birth-star was the light of burning plains.*]—Alluding to the miseries that attended the American civil war.

[2] P. 60. Cougar, the American tiger.

[3] P. 62. *The Mammoth comes.*]—That I am justified in making the Indian chief allude to the mammoth as an emblem of terror and destruction, will be seen by the authority quoted below. Speaking of the mammoth, or big buffalo, Mr. Jefferson states, that a tradition is preserved among the Indians of that animal still existing in the northern parts of America.

"A delegation of warriors from the Delaware tribe having visited the governor of Virginia during the revolution, on matters of business, the governor asked them some questions relative to their country, and, among others, what they knew, or had heard, of the animal whose bones were found at the Salt-licks, on the Ohio. Their chief speaker immediately put himself into an attitude of oratory, and with a pomp suited to what he had conceived the elevation of his subject, informed him, that it was a tradition handed down from their fathers, that in ancient times a herd of these tremendous animals came to the Big-bone-licks, and began an universal destruction of the bear, deer, elk, buffalo, and other animals which had been created for the use of the Indians. That the great Man above, looking down and seeing this, was so enraged, that he seized his lightning, descended on the earth, seated himself on a neighbouring mountain on a rock, on which his seat, and the prints of his feet, are still to be seen, and hurled his bolts among them, till the whole were slaughtered except the big bull, who, presenting his forehead to the shafts, shook them off as they fell, but, missing one, at length it wounded him in the side, whereon, springing round, he bounded over the Ohio, over the Wabash, the Illinois, and finally over the great lakes, where he is living at this day."—*Jefferson's Notes on Virginia.*

[4] P. 62. *Scorning to wield the hatchet for his bribe,*
*'Gainst Brandt himself I went to battle forth.*]

I took the character of Brandt, in the poem of Gertrude, from the common Histories of England, all of which represented him as a bloody and bad man (even among savages), and chief agent in the horrible desolation of Wyoming. Some years after this poem appeared, the son of Brandt, a most interesting and intelligent youth, came over to England, and I formed an acquaintance with him, on which I still look back with pleasure. He appealed to my sense of honour and justice, on his own part and on that of his sister, to retract the unfair aspersions which, unconscious of their unfairness, I had cast on his father's memory.

He then referred me to documents, which completely satisfied me that the common accounts of Brandt's cruelties at Wyoming, which I had found in books of Travels and in Adolphus's and similar Histories of England, were gross errors, and that in point of fact Brandt was not even present at that scene of desolation.

It is, unhappily, to Britons and Anglo-Americans that we must refer the chief blame in this horrible business. I published a letter expressing this belief in the *New Monthly Magazine*, in the year 1822, to which I must refer the reader—if he has any curiosity on the subject—for an antidote to my fanciful description of Brandt. Among other expressions to young Brandt, I made use of the following words:—"Had I learnt all this of your father when I was writing my poem, he should not have figured in it as the hero of mischief." It was but bare justice to say thus much of a Mohawk Indian, who spoke English eloquently, and was thought capable of having written a history of the Six Nations. I ascertained, also, that he often strove to mitigate the cruelty of Indian warfare. The name of Brandt, therefore, remains in my poem a pure and declared character of fiction.

[5] P. 62. *To whom nor relative nor blood remains;*
*No!—not a kindred drop that runs in human veins.*]

Every one who recollects the specimen of Indian eloquence given in the speech of Logan, a Mingo chief, to the Governor of Virginia, will perceive that I have attempted to paraphrase its concluding and most striking expression—"There runs not a drop of my blood in the veins of any living creature." The similar salutation of the fictitious personage in my story, and the real Indian orator, makes it surely allowable to borrow such an expression; and if it appears, as it cannot but appear, to less advantage than in the original, I beg the reader to reflect how difficult it is to transpose such exquisitely simple words, without sacrificing a portion of their effect.

In the spring of 1774, a robbery and murder were committed on an inhabitant of the frontiers of Virginia, by two Indians of the Shawanee tribe. The neighbouring whites, according to their custom, undertook to punish this outrage in a summary manner. Colonel Cresap, a man infamous for the many murders he had committed on those much injured people, collected a party and proceeded down the Kanaway in quest of vengeance; unfortunately a canoe with women and children, with one man only, was seen coming from the opposite shore, unarmed, and unsuspecting an attack from the whites. Cresap and his party concealed themselves on the bank of the river, and the moment the canoe reached the shore, singled out their objects, and at one fire killed every person in it. This happened to be the family of Logan, who had long been distinguished as a friend to the whites. This unworthy return provoked his vengeance; he accordingly signalised himself in the war which ensued. In the autumn of the same year a decisive battle was fought at the mouth of the great Kanaway, in which the collected forces of the Shawanees, Mingoes, and Delawares were defeated by a detachment of the Virginian militia. The Indians sued for peace. Logan, however, disdained to be seen among the suppliants; but lest the sincerity of a treaty should be disturbed from which so distinguished a chief abstracted himself, he sent, by a messenger, the following speech to be delivered to Lord Dunmore.

"I appeal to any white man if ever he entered Logan's cabin hungry, and he gave him not to eat; if ever he came cold and hungry, and he clothed him not. During the course of the last long and bloody war, Logan remained idle in his cabin, an advocate for peace. Such was my love for the whites, that my countrymen pointed as they passed, and said, Logan is the friend of the white men. I have even thought to have lived with you, but for the injuries of one man. Colonel Cresap, the last spring, in cold blood murdered all the relations of Logan, even my women and children.

"There runs not a drop of my blood in the veins of any living creature.—This called on me for revenge.—I have fought for it.—I have killed many.—I have fully glutted my vengeance.—For my country I rejoice at the beams of peace—but do not harbour a thought that mine is the joy of fear.—Logan never felt fear.—He will not turn on his heel to save his life.—Who is there to mourn for Logan? not one!"—*Jefferson's Notes on Virginia.*

THE END.

LONDON:
PRINTED BY RICHARD CLAY,
BREAD STREET HILL.

www.ingramcontent.com/pod-product-compliance
Lightning Source LLC
LaVergne TN
LVHW010743120826
845150LV00009B/2112

* 9 7 8 1 4 2 5 5 0 8 0 9 8 *